The Cheltenham Experience

by
Miriam Harrison & Shirley Alexander

The Devil's Chimney a famous Cotswold landmark over looking the town of Cheltenham Spa

Published by
REARDON PUBLISHING
56, Upper Norwood Street, Leckhampton,
Cheltenham, Glos GL53 0DU

Copyright 1997
A joint publication between
Reardon Publishing and Corinium Publications

Written and Researched
by
Miriam Harrison & Shirley Alexander

ISBN 1 873877 24 2

Layout & Design
Nicholas Reardon

Illustrations & Drawings
Peter Reardon

Maps by Shirley Alexander & Andy Green

Front cover photo Neptune's Fountain
Nicholas Reardon

Other photos Miriam Harrison

Printed by
STOATE & BISHOP (Printers) Ltd
Cheltenham, Glos

The Cheltenham Experience

Cheltenham, the town under the hill, grew from the small village beside the river Chelt which was first mentioned in ecclesiastical circles in 773 AD, to the town of outstanding importance it is today. Edward the Confessor was the first recorded Lord of the Manor in the eleventh century. He imposed a hunting tax on the people and compelled them to supply him annually with "3000 loaves for the dogs". The town was granted the right to hold a market in 1226 by King Henry III. It became a borough in 1313 but it was as a spa town, in the eighteenth century, and later as a centre for learning, that its fame became international. The town coat of arms, containing the cross of Edward the Confessor, was given to the town in 1887 along with the motto "Salubritas et Eruditio" meaning "Health and Learning", the twin hall-marks of the town.

General agriculture was the mainstay of the area. In the 17th century Cheltenham and Winchcombe were the country's most important centres for the illegal growing of tobacco. The mild, damp climate favoured the healthy growth of the fragrant nicotiana in the Cotswolds.

The medicinal properties of the waters of Cheltenham were first discovered in 1716 when the activities of the local pigeons were noted as they pecked at the encrusted salt around the spring. The owner of this piece of land, William Mason, built a thatched shed over the spring and charged people a fee to drink the special mineral waters drawn from the well. The spa was inherited by Mason's daughter who later married Henry Skillicorne, a retired sea captain. He had the business acumen to turn the spring into a most successful commercial operation. Skillicorne went on to build an assembly room and to plant an avenue lined with elm trees, to enhance the walk up to the well. The present Ladies College was built on the former site of this well. As the spring water grew in popularity it soon became clear that this single supply was inadequate to meet the need of the many visitors. Other land owners in the vicinity prospected for water by sinking well holes and other sources of mineral waters were discovered. After a visit to Cheltenham by the reigning monarch, King George III, in 1788, the Old Well, as the Skillicorne spa was called, became known as the King's Well. The King's daily sampling of the waters throughout his stay in Cheltenham, which lasted from July 12th until the royal party left on August 16th 1788, firmly placed Cheltenham on the fashionable spa circuit for a very long time. John Goding writes in his Norman's History of Cheltenham about the changes in the town,*'In all probability it would have continued to this day in that obsolete condition, had not Providence ordained that these health-restoring springs should be brought to light and their virtues applied to remove the bitter sting of affliction.'*

Cheltenham is also famous for its many festivals: horse racing, cricket, music and literature. The internationally famous Cheltenham National Hunt three day festival, including the Cheltenham Gold Cup, is held annually in March. Racing was first established in 1819 under the patronage of the Duke of Gloucester, at Cleeve Hill. As the popularity of flat racing waned and the steeplechase took over, organised largely by Colonel Berkeley, master of the hunt. In 1844 it became an annual event held in Prestbury Park. The "Hall of Fame" is open all year and tells the story of steeplechasing. The cricket festival has been an annual event since 1877, and was originally held in honour of W.G.Grace and his eleven. Taking place in the beautiful grounds of Cheltenham College in July, it is the oldest cricket festival in Britain. Also in July is the International Music Festival with its focus on contemporary composers. On the fringes of this festival there is jazz, rock, film and dance music with street entertainment and fireworks. The Literary Festival in October was the first of its kind to offer a platform for talented writers to parade their skills. Nowadays it attracts famous names in modern literature including writers, actors and poets of international fame.

Point 1. The Promenade (see centre map)

We begin our circular walk at the top of the fashionable Promenade, starting outside the Midland Bank building shown on the map in the centre fold of the book. There is also a quiz in the centrefold. The Midland Bank and the adjoining buildings are of particular interest as they are of French Renaissance style and very impressive.

We pause here for a moment and invite you to step back into Regency times with us. Imagine yourself sweeping along the Promenade in a carriage, drawn by a perfectly matched pair of horses, on your way to sample the healing mineral waters of the Imperial Spa. The fine Promenade, started in 1818 was, by 1826 a carriage drive with wide gravelled walks on each side. Many of the buildings in this treelined avenue are Regency and we hope it might amuse you to know that in Regency times, the Promenade allowed only wealthy subscribers to parade and laid down a ruling which said that 'no servant of any description is allowed to come on the walk during the hours of the promenade, or into the gardens at any time ... dogs are likewise prohibited'. Thankfully things are much more relaxed today and we can all enjoy parading along the Promenade.

As we move towards point 2 on the map we suggest you look up to the first floors, above the various shops, to admire the balconies and the fine stuccoed friezes.

Point 2. Cavendish House

As you walk towards the pedestrian section of the Promenade glance across the road to your right to catch a glimpse of the work by Dame Barbara Hepworth. It is on the wall of a commercial building and is called 'Themes and Variations'. Look across the road at the Hooper building which boasts a most outstanding facade and was built in 1823. It was first the home of the painter Millet. It later became the Imperial Hotel and in 1856, the Imperial Club. This exclusive club was very selective and only opened its doors to resident Noblemen and Gentlemen. A mixed history, which included being used as the town's main Post Office, culminated in 1987 as the handsome retail establishment of today. Number 21, on the corner of the Promenade, was the Christian Reading Rooms.

As you move further down the Promenade look across the road to admire the Municipal Office buildings with their Ionic columns.

The Municipal Offices in the Promenade

This was once known as the Harward Building, named after the man who developed the site. It was designed by George Underwood and built after the style of the Louvre, between 1823 and 1825. There are three statues in the gardens in front of the building. The first commemorates the South African campaign. The second is the war memorial and the last is to commemorate a local hero, Edward Adrian Wilson, who died with Scott in Antarctica, in 1912. At the far end of the buildings is the Neptune fountain. This is said to be fed by the river Chelt which runs under the town. When we come back down the road we will take a closer look at the fountain and the grand Municipal Building.

Point 3. The Town Hall

Turn into Imperial Square to see the Edwardian baroque Town Hall designed by Frederick William Waller, built in 1902-3. It was opened by the Mayor to celebrate the start of King Edward VII's reign. Many of the functions of the former assembly rooms are carried out at the Town Hall. The literary, music and drama festivals are performed here and are considered to be very much part of the "Cheltenham Experience".

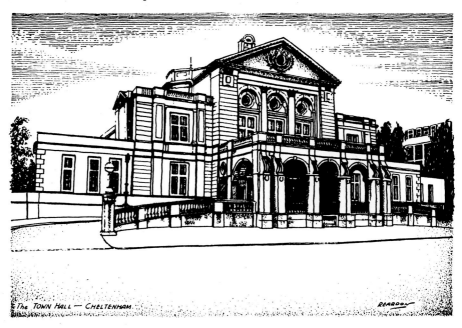

The Town Hall

It is here that the waters can be drunk up to the present day. Cross over the road, past the Town Hall, and walk up the left side of Imperial Square noting the Imperial Gardens on your right. We will return here shortly. There are many terraces of fine Regency buildings here. Many of them have original ironwork railings at the first floor, with the famous heart and honeysuckle design that is often repeated in the town. At the end of this terrace turn left. Facing you will be three unique cottages in Trafalgar Street. Nelson Cottage, with its outstanding tiny front garden, Nelson Lodge and Nelson Villa have exquisite balconies with classical filigree wrought ironwork. As you face the cottages turn right walk to the top of Trafalgar Street and cross over Montpellier Spa Road. Turn left and walk to the corner before looking across at the impressive Clarmont Lodge.

One of the Town Hall Urns where you can try the waters

This is one of the finest examples of Regency architecture in the town. It stands at the junction of Victoria Walk and with Montpellier Spa Road. Now walk back the short distance to the Imperial Square gardens.

Point 4. The Imperial Gardens

These gardens are a riot of colour in the summer months. Enjoy the formal floral beds and the fountain. Glance across towards the rear of the Town Hall, and walk down to look at the tiny secluded garden situated there. It contains a bust of Captain Skillicorne and a modern statue.

This strange little 'Oriental Lady' statue
can be seen in the secluded garden

The Winter Gardens stood on this spot but sadly fell into disrepair. They were demolished in 1940. During the first world war the interior was used to assemble planes, and later the same area was used for car assembly. We can still enjoy some reminder of the gardens as the layout of the paths in the Imperial Gardens show where the entrances to the Winter Gardens would have been. Indeed the refreshment area uses the base of one of the former towers, so in its own way the memory of this mini Crystal Palace lives on. Across the road a wonderful view can be had of the many interesting and unique villas.

Point 5. The Queens Hotel

The impressive Queens Hotel, with the facade of six Corinthian pillars is modelled on the temple of Jupiter in Rome. Built on the site of the Imperial Spa, by the Jearrad Brothers, it was opened in 1838. Many guests of distinction have stayed here, notably King Edward VII, and it has continued to attract many celebrities and public figures of today. Look out for the Crimean War Memorial and canon housing. The canon was removed in 1940 to aid the war effort. Rumour has it that the canon was taken to a seaside town and is still on display there today. Go past the front of the Hotel and cross the road using the central refuge to assist you. Continue up to Montpellier Walk.

Point 6. The parade of shops at Montpellier

Montpellier is named after the spa town of Montpellier in the south of France where many British people were interned during the Napoleonic Wars. The area became known as the continental quarter of the town. The road widens and the shops on the right are set back on a slip road. This unique row of shops, with their balustraded parapets, were designed by J B Papworth. Here you can view the life-sized statues called Caryatids, which were set up between the shops in 1842-3. Now cross the road to the gardens opposite.

Point 7. Montpellier Gardens

Montpellier Gardens were added soon after the opening of the Montpellier Spa in 1809 to provide an ornamental pleasure ground. This was a venue for many social events. Imagine standing and watching the balloon flights so enjoyed in the 1830s and 1840s. Half way across the gardens there is a broad avenue that leads down to the bandstand. It was built in 1895 and has iron railings inset with pictures of a female head. Some people thought these represented Queen Victoria but in fact they were one of the standard patterns from the ironwork pattern book. Renovation was carried out in 1994. We can still to this day see the remains of the open air theatre now used as a fitness centre, albeit with some modern additions. In its heyday it would have looked very pretty with striped awnings in the Edwardian manner. Continue further on to the statue of King William IV. The statue was erected in 1832 to mark the passing of the Reform Bill and was paid for by public subscription. It was moved to its present site in 1920.

1st Optional Spur. The Continental Spur

Here we give you the chance to enjoy this continental section of Cheltenham before you rejoin our circular walk.

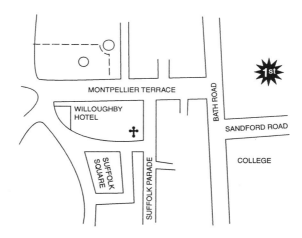

Turn to the right as you face the statue and take the path that leads up to Montpellier Terrace, past the end tennis court. Cross the road at the controlled crossing and walk to your left, cross over Suffolk Parade and Montpellier Grove, down to the Bath Road. There are many examples of Regency buildings on the right as you walk down the road. Look out for number 91 the house where Edward Wilson was born in 1872. At the traffic lights at the end of the road you will see, on the opposite corner of the staggered junction, the College Buildings. Explore these at your leisure and return to Montpellier Terrace. Retrace your steps up to the second turning on the left and turn into Suffolk Parade. In this road there is an interesting variety of shops, a little continental quarter with antique shops and a wine bar. Turn right into Suffolk Square past the Victorian Gothic Church of St James, designed by Papworth and Jenkins, and then look up at the ironwork on the terrace to your right. Turn right at the end of terrace. The house on the end, now the Willoughby House Hotel, was once the farmhouse to the once famous Gallipot Estate. Continue around to the front of Montpellier Terrace by Glendale House and turn right. Walk back to the controlled crossing and into the Montpellier Gardens and the statue of King William IV.

You are now back on the circular walk.

Return to the bandstand. If you have children with you there is a small play area close by set aside for their pleasure. Even if you are unattended do walk up past the play area as the path that leads back to the road affords one of the best views of the Rotunda and, as you approach the road, of the parade of shops designed by Papworth. Admire their ironwork railings and stone balustrades. Cross the road onto the central island where you will find a statue of King Edward VII in uniform helping a poor girl. It is set on an oval granite base and was once a fountain.

Lion's Head drinking fountain on the King Edward VII's statue and once believed to dispense spa waters to thirsty travellers

Point 8. The Rotunda

The Montpellier Spa was opened in 1809 by Henry Thomson as a rival spa. The first construction was a wooden building with a colonnade. This structure was replaced in stone, designed by G A Underwood, with the lion taking pride of place on the parapet. Pearson Thomson, Henry's son, asked John B Papworth, the famous London architect to add the dome in 1825-26. This magnificent Rotunda has similar proportions to Rome's Pantheon. It now forms part of Lloyds Bank but you can still enter during banking hours to view the beautiful, and recently renovated, dome from inside.

Walk up the road, leaving the Lloyds Bank building behind you and follow the line of shops around. Before you walk down Montpellier Street cross over to the Bank of Scotland building, Lauriston House. This was once the home of Dr Thomas Richardson Colledge, the founder of the Medical Missionary Society. This is a good vantage point to view the Gordon Lamp, erected early in 1885 by public subscription. Shortly afterwards General Gordon was killed in Khartoum and it was decided to dedicate the lamp to his memory. The base of the lamp is made from red and grey granite and was made by Fraser and Son of Aberdeen. Note also the cherubs adorning this impressive lamp. Also admire the Regency bow of the Montpellier Wine Bar Building and the archway to Royal Parade Mews. Look out for the stones jutting out at wheel level. In Regency times they prevented damage to the archway from the carriages. This was once the entrance to the Old Well from this end of town.

Original entrance to the old well on the corner of Royal Parade Mews

2nd Optional spur. The Architectural Spur

This is a chance for you to look at some the best architectural crescents and terraces in Cheltenham, before returning to the circular walk.

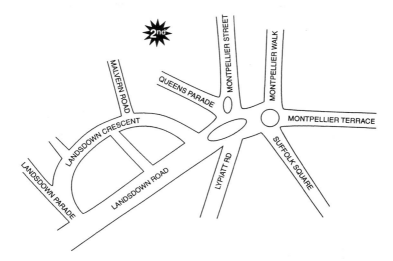

Walk beyond the Bank of Scotland building towards the Gordon Lamp. Cross over Lansdown Crescent and walk down Lansdown Road. On the right there are several terraces to admire and on the other side of the road, many villas which are typical of the town. Cross over Lansdown Walk and continue to the end of the road. Turn right into Lansdown Parade and bear right into the magnificent Lansdown Crescent. This was begun in 1828 by J B Papworth but only number 2 was built to his design. The terrace was continued after 1831 by the architects R W and C Jearrard. Building was still going on as late as 1850. The incredible front elevation of this convex facade is over a quarter of a mile long. It cannot conveniently be seen from a distance and consequently fails to give a true impression of its simplicity and size. Admire the double porches with their Doric columns. In the centre of this architectural landscape there is a peaceful haven of green, allowing time for a leisurely break. Look beyond the gardens and see the unique terraces and villas in Lansdown Parade. Cross the road at Lansdown Court, an Italianate building and turn into Malvern Road in order to view Landsdown Terrace. Many people believe this is to be the most important terrace in the town. The majority of the houses have now been renovated. Continue along Lansdown Crescent and return to the Bank of Scotland building.   You are now back on the circular walk.

Point 9. Montpellier Street

Cross over and walk down Montpellier Street. You will be able to see through the narrow shops to catch a glimpse of the gardens beyond. Look across the road to the wonderful facades above the shops, noting the chemist shop with its Victorian sign. John Nevil Maskelyne, the magician lived here. He worked as a watchmaker and when he was asked to repair an artificial limb, it occurred to him how mediums of the day were able to produce table rappings. He exposed their deceptions in March 1865 when he visited an exhibition of spiritualism. This aroused his interest in illusionism and magic and he built an automata, a magic box, which is still used by Paul Daniels and other magicians to the present day. At the end of the row of shops, on the left side of the road, is a new courtyard development with some interesting little shops. It is well worth stopping to look around.

Part of Cheltenham Ladies College seen from Montpellier Street

Glance down at the side of the Cheltenham Ladies College with its dome and clock tower. Walk back into Montpellier Walk, with the Queen's Hotel in front of you, turn left and make your way back down the Promenade.

14

Point 10. The Promenade Villas

Walk back down on the left side of the road. Glance across at the Imperial Gardens. You are now walking past some villas. Number 133 is attributed to J B Papworth with its stuccoed facade and the individual tented canopies over the first floor windows. Number 129 is described as the best Regency villa in the town. Numbers 125 to 127 are fine early Nineteenth Century buildings with six pilasters with composite caps. Numbers 99 to 119 are Grade II listed buildings and are described as one of the best regency terraces in Cheltenham. Note their excellent wrought iron work trellis verandas and tented canopies to the first floor balconies.   These are based on the star pattern, one of the more unusual motifs. Take the spur or cross over St George's Road to the fountain.

Neptune's Fountain in the Promenade this wonderful drawing
shows how Neptune once looked with his original trident

A Looking at fine stonework - Hooper Bolton is your clue.
Are you game to **hunt** the view ?
ANSWER _ _ _ _ _ _ _ _ _ _ _ _ _ _ _ _ _ _

B Six bright sentinals, fancy that!
You may go in to have a chat. What ?
ANSWER _ _ _ _ _ _ _ _ _ _ _ _ _ _ _ _

C Do not move far, now here's a sight, a ring
of pigeons, not in flight. What and how many ?
ANSWER _ _ _ _ _ _ _ _ _ _ _ _ _ _ _ _ _ _

D So now go into Imperial Road and the Town Hall
soon you will behold. Floral garlands greet our eye,
on stone uprights, not too high. How many ?
ANSWER _ _ _ _ _ _ _ _ _ _ _ _ _ _ _ _ _ _

E Fit for a Queen is our next clue,
Crowns for me and you and you. How Many ?
ANSWER _ _ _ _ _ _ _ _ _ _ _ _ _ _ _ _ _ _ _

F At Montpellier shops I'm fishing here for a clue,
she stands between not one but two. What and where ?
ANSWER _ _ _ _ _ _ _ _ _ _ _ _ _ _ _ _

G Stroll by the shop which you think is the best. We
ask with interest, are these Caryatids the same as the rest ?
ANSWER _ _ _ _ _ _ _ _ _ _ _ _ _ _ _ _ _ _ _

H From Montpellier Gardens look across and around.
A flying animal, not on the ground. What ?
ANSWER _ _ _ _ _ _ _ _ _ _ _ _ _ _ _ _ _ _

I Follow your map to Montpellier Street - a golden symbol
how elite! Beware it may crush or grind, so you ought'er
name it as a _ _ _ _ _ and _ _ _ _ _ _ ?
ANSWER _ _ _ _ _ _ _ _ _ _ _ _ _ _ _ _

J Walk to the end of Montpellier Street, now cross
back to the " Prom " for another treat. Look and lean
but do not swim ! How many hooves **rest** on the rim?
ANSWER _ _ _ _ _ _ _ _ _ _ _ _ _ _ _ _ _ _

K A building based on the Louvre ?
On the front a crest with pigeons, how unique!
And symetrical arches, it's the number we seek.
How many and what building ?
ANSWER _ _ _ _ _ _ _ _ _ _ _ _ _ _ _ _ _

Map 8

BOOTS

HIGH STREET

ST. GEORGES PLACE

ROYAL CRESCENT

ROYAL WELL WALK

PROMENADE

LADIES COLLEGE

MONTPELLIER STREET

MONTPELLIER WALK

GORDON LAMP

KEY

❋ Park
✝ Church
𝒾 Information
P Car Park
T Toilet

L Into Crescent Place we now shall go, the _ _ _ _   _ _ _ _ _ House is now on show. To give you yet another clue, both **Lion** and **Unicorn** are on view.   Name this important building.

Answer _

M A red brick Palace with no front door: but it's not lived in we are quite sure.   Name the building ?

ANSWER _

N Built in 1887, a **bookish** building vast and grand. A bust upon the top does stand ? Lost quill perhaps! Name both

ANSWER _

O We wander on with nimble feet and soon we stroll down the High Street. In **principle** you might agree, three pretty tiers times two to see.   What feature ?

ANSWER _

P In this most impressive fiscal building : - A place to earn could be a clue, but how many **Urns** are there in view ?   Set your sights high !

ANSWER _

Q You are not **Before** or **Behind**. It is **time** you checked your **compass point** on this red and yellow streaky bacon joint. What and where ? Dutch influence!

ANSWER _

R We are now in Rodney Road,   you should be in a confident mode.   In letters high **he** shouts his name, above baptist Church of Cambray fame.   Give the name.

ANSWER _

S Wisteria climbing on the balcony wall, but it's _ _ _ _ _ _   _ _ _ _ _ not Rodney Hall.

ANSWER _ _ _ _ _ _ _ _ _ _ _ _ _ _ _ _ _ _ _

T A Royal Arcade ? Yes that's the trick - it is helping to make Cheltenham tick ! The last quiz clue here , so make a wish standing under the _ _ _ _ _ _ _ Fish.

ANSWER _

Find the answers to the quiz at the back of the book!

15

WINCHCOMBE STREET

4th

GH STREET

18

17

✝

16

5th

RODNEY ROAD

CAMBRAY PLACE

20 19

T

ACE

T STREET

SQUARE

3

IMPERIAL SQUARE

TRAFALGAR STREET

❋

L SQUARE

NTPELLIER SPA ROAD

❋

1st

BANDSTAND

ELLIER TERRACE

3rd Optional spur. The Victorian Spur

Which includes the Cheltenham Ladies College and Bayshill Road.

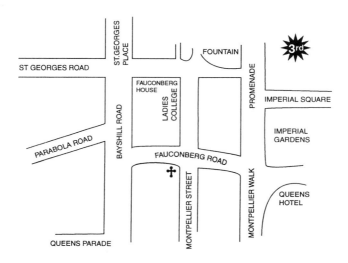

Walk up St George's Road, past the Ladies College. Next door is Fauconberg House. This house was named after Lord Fauconberg. He was a gentleman-in-waiting to King George III and was credited with inviting the King to stay at his Cheltenham home, now sadly demolished. This visit subsequently made Cheltenham Spa internationally famous. Admire the wonderful castiron gate piers, gates and railings, particularly noting the authemion design and antefix-ae. Now turn into Bayshill Road. Walk the length of the road, cross over at the top and return on the other side of the road. Look at the cast ironwork, the difference between it and wrought iron can be clearly seen. Admire the vitruvian scroll in the cast ironwork railings. Villas and terraces, so typical of Cheltenham, abound. On the corner of Parabola Road there is a hexagonal Penfold letter box with the cast crest and the lettering,V R. Return and cross Bayshill Road at the traffic lights. Cross over St George's Road and turn right towards the Promenade. Glance across the road at the Ladies College and cross over Royal Well Road, past the side of Royscot House, to the Neptune Fountain.

You have now returned to the circular walk.

Point 11. The Neptune Fountain

This fountain depicts Neptune being drawn by sea horses and was designed by Joseph Hall, the Borough Engineer. He was said to have been influenced in his design choice by the Fontana Di Trevi in Rome. The Neptune Fountain was constructed by R L Boulton, the local sculptor, in 1893. Stop to enjoy the sight of this ornate fountain spraying the waters of the elusive river Chelt.

The town coat of arms, complete with pigeons, sits above the main entrance of the magnificent Municipal Building. The Tourist Information Office is within this terrace offering a multitude of local information. Look at the steps leading up to the front doors. On the third set from the right, you will notice marble set into the edge of the treads. This is the last remaining relic from Regency times when the gentry rolled out the red carpet to show they were in residence. Turn left after the Municipal building into Clarence Parade. Cross over the road and walk past the impressive Promenade House on the corner of Post Office Lane. Cross Clarence Parade and straight ahead of you is the Royal Crescent.

Point 12. The Royal Crescent and the John Dower Building

View the Royal Crescent. At number1 and again at numbers 9 and 10, the evidence of gas lighting can be clearly seen in the ornamental ironwork. Turn into Crescent Place. Cross over the road at the John Dower building where you will see some interesting ironwork on the balconies of the first floor. The building is now the home of the Countryside Commission, but was once Liddell's Boarding House, where Adelade, Duchess of Clarence stayed in 1827, hence the royal crest above the door.

Point 13. The Art Gallery and Museum

Turn left into Clarence Street, glance across the road to see the town's Art Gallery and Museum. Walk to the corner, past the Church of St Matthew's. Cross over St George's Place and Clarence Street to view the most unusual electricity sub-station designed to look like the Strozzi Palace, Florence. The Cheltenham Civic Society has placed a plaque on the wall. If you wish, cross over St George's Place and walk up the side of the library to look at the house where Dr Jenner, the pioneer of vaccinations, once lived. The Cheltenham Civic Society has placed a plaque on the wall of the house. Cross over St George's Place to the view the impressive library frontage.

If time permits a visit, the Art Gallery and Museum comes highly recommended; admission is free. There you will see imaginative displays of how people lived in the past, internationally acclaimed collections from the arts and crafts movement of William Morris and his contemporaries and a notable collection of Old Master paintings donated by Baron De Ferrieres. On the second floor of the Art Gallery and Museum, in rc om 1, on the left as you enter, is a fine oil painting of The Plough Inn by John C Maggs. It was painted in 1820. This important building has been reconstructed in the High Street as the Regent Arcade and will be instantly recognisable from this notable work.

When you come out of the Art Gallery and Museum, turn left and then turn left again, into Well Walk and St Mary's Churchyard. Here we suggest you turn around and glance back to imagine the splendid well walk, which was 20 feet wide (approx 6. metres) lined with elegant elm trees. For the Centenary Fete of the Royal Old Well Walk, in August 1838, hosts of fairy lights formed a magnificent avenue of arches as part of their celebrations.

Point 14.   St Mary's Church

The oldest building in the town is, of course, the Church of St Mary's, dating back to the 12th century, when it was built by the Abbot of Cirencester. Veer right and take the right fork towards the South Porch. Before you enter the church, glance up to see the "Church Watch Dog", which is a carved stop to the hood mould of the window on the left side of the porch entrance. Walk into the medieval Church. It is open between the hours of 11.00a.m. and 3.00p.m. most days. As you enter the Church look to your left at the stained glass window showing the last supper; it is clear and colourful. Notice Judas Iscariot's dark halo among all the bright gold ones of Jesus and the other disciples. The food on the table also deserves a second look as it does not appear to be the typical food eaten in Palestine in the first century. Most of the stained glass dates from late Victorian times. The delicate stone tracery is of great beauty and holds the eye. The many and varied designs around the Church date back from the fourteenth century. Move to the centre of the Church. From this vantage point you will be able to see the communion table and the window above. Turn and admire the window at the back of the Church. Walk to the far side of the Church, in line with the door through which you entered, and you will see the oldest part of the building. The little gallery above the baptistery was once the school begun by George Townsend in 1680. It was used for more than one hundred years as a small charity school run by the Church to teach poor children of the parish to write.

At one point the ageing schoolmaster had to be carried up the narrow external stairs by his pupils. The school moved in 1847 and became part of the National School in Devonshire Street. Now look to the front of the building to admire the beautiful rose window with its deliberate, or perhaps not, mistake within its pattern. As you walk towards the rose window, squeeze in between the pews to the left of the window, to see a poignant inscription about a woman who was poisoned by a servant. Turn again and walk towards the nave. Here you may go forward to look more closely at the communion table and the choir stalls. Return and continue through the arch. Here you will see many inscriptions in the marble panels, a notable one being the epitaph to Captain Henry Skillicorne, believed to be the longest in the country.

The famous Rose window in the North Transept
of the Parish Church of St Mary's

The Rev. Francis Close was the "incumbent" of St Mary's from 1826 to 1856. This thirty year period was know as the "Close season". Alfred, Lord Tennyson dubbed him "The Pope of Cheltenham" which was ironic as he was a leading member of the evangelical movement of the time. He was a champion of the rights of the poor and worked for educational opportunities in the town. In an out-spoken attack from the pulpit, the Rev Close strongly condemned what he thought was an excess of merriment in Cheltenham by saying:

"The font of health and mirth
The merriest sick resort on earth"

Before you leave the Church, may we recommend the available leaflets and postcards. The booklet entitled "Parish Church of St Mary, Cheltenham", is most informative and reasonably priced.

Leave the Church by the same door and turn left. There are some market measures set in the pathway but you will need sharp eyes to see them. They are brass and about three inches (7cm) long, running at right angles to the edge of the path. The first is by a pathway leading to a tiny door as you walk towards the front of the church. The second is by the corner buttress, about one foot (30cm) from the edge of the path. The last one, on the other side of the pathway that continues around the Church, is opposite a tree. These marks were used in the measurement of rope and cloth. It was thought that if the measure was in the church yard the traders would give honest lengths! Leave the Church grounds by the widest path and go past a public house. Now turn right along a little alleyway which leads from the quiet oasis of calm to the hustle and bustle of the High Street.

Point 15. The High Street and its buildings

As you proceed along the High Street, the commercial heart of the town, there are many building of historical interest and you are invited to take a step back in time. Walk past the Boots building on your left. Look up above the shop fronts to the first floors, many of them are worth noting. On the right hand side of the walkway is the Burton's building with its Art Deco style. On the corner of Regent Street stands a white building with its stylish swags in stone work. The Marks and Spencer building, on the left, was once the George Hotel, one of the oldest coaching Inns in Cheltenham. The Lamb Inn was on the corner of Winchcombe Street, and this building still exists today. Cheltenham was a town built mainly of brick because so much suitable clay was available. It was the practice at that time for bricks to be made from the clay dug on the site of the building for which they were required. The new houses were faced with stone, plaster or stucco, linking them harmoniously one to another.

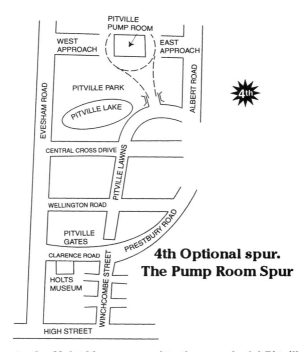

4th Optional spur.
The Pump Room Spur

Here we take you to the Holst Museum and to the wonderful Pittville gardens and pump room. Walk up Winchcombe Street and cross over St Margarets Road. Continue up to Clarence Road and turn left. The Holst Museum is number 4, on the left. It is dedicated to Gustav Holst's life and works. His grand piano can be seen on the ground floor. The is an excellent chance to feel the atmosphere of Regency and Victorian life in this well maintained, three storeyed, small Regency house. Leave the Museum and turn right. Cross over Clarence Road and walk up to the Pittville Gates. Go through the gates into the beautiful gardens of the Pittville estate. Walk up the road known as Pittville Lawn and continue up the long garden admiring the terraces and villas on the right hand side of the road. Number 27, Kenilworth House is a fine example of early nineteenth century architecture with Corinthian pilasters through both floors and a central stone porch with Corinthian columns. The terrace, number 29 to 37, was designed by the architect John Forbes. The gate post, to the entrance of number 37 has a tree growing through it. Pittville Lodge number 39, is described as being "a villa of good proportions with first floor Doric pilasters and dentil entablature." 45 to 53 have Ionic order through the first and second floors and 55 is a stucco villa. Numbers 59 to 67 are similar to 55 with wrought iron balconies at the first floor. Regency Lodge is number 69 and it has Corinthian pilasters.

Walk through into Pittville gardens, over the little bridge and catch your first glimpse of the magnificent classically inspired Pump Room with its dome. It is open each day except Tuesday's between 11.00am and 4.00pm in the winter and between 11.00am and 4.30pm in the summer. Entry is free into the gardens and also to the pump room, where you may go to taste the waters. (Concerts, weddings and performances may restrict access) The building of the pump room was watched by the Duke of Wellington during his visit in 1825. He spoke with many of the workmen who were veterans of Waterloo.

The Pittville Pump Rooms

The building was used by the American army in the second world war and was found to have dry rot. At one time it was thought the building would have to be pulled down but it was saved by public subscription and re-opened by the 7th Duke of Wellington in 1960. The grounds are extensive and there is a small zoological area with aviaries and a children's play ground within a dog free compound. For your further enjoyment there is an ornamental boating lake, an 18 hole pitch and putt course, play tennis, skate board and rollerblade facilities and, for the very energetic, an orienteering track. Look around at your leisure and return by crossing over the bridge and walking down the long garden into Winchcombe Street and at the High Street turn left. You have now returned to the circular walk.

Continue down the High Street into the pedestrian area. Look up again, above the shop fronts, to see the various architectural styles.

5th Optional spur.
The Sandford Park and the River Chelt Spur

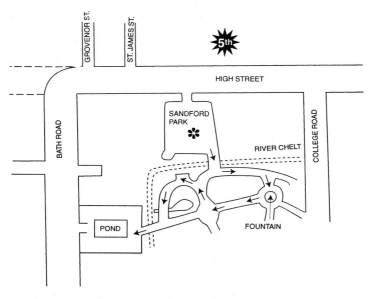

At the end of the pedestrianised area keep to the left side and cross the road at the controlled crossing. Look over to the oak beamed fifteenth century building, called the Restoration Inn, on the corner of Grovenor Street. Continue to walk on the right hand side of the road. Look across the road to the corner of St James Street. Here is an fine example of a Victorian pub, with a green tiled exterior, called Cactus Jacks. Look particularly at the entrance porch. Further down the road at number 37 is O'Hagen's Bar. This was once the Old Swan Inn. For 200 years it was the first Inn to welcome travellers arriving at the London end of Cheltenham High Street. Look down the cobbled archway to see an old gas light and a canopied shelter. Turn right and enter through the iron gateway into Sandford Park. Pergolas to left and right and a lion headed fountain, at the top of this delightful entrance, greet the eye. Take the left path, walk over the bridge and turn left. The river Chelt flows through the park.

Keep the green railings to your left and continue down until you see the rococo fountain, through the shrubbery, and turn right towards it. Glance across the road to a vast recreational area which gives access to the Sandford Park Lido. Walk three quarters of the way around the fountain anti-clockwise and

25

continue towards some shell like pieces of public art and the Friendship circle. These pieces of public art are by the sculptor Neville Gabie who was born in Johannesburg South Africa in 1959. The philosophy behind public art was to improve the environment by creating works of art appropriate to the particular location. In the middle of the circle turn right, walk a few paces and on the left you will follow the roughly paved path. To enjoy the tumbling water continue walking with the green railings on your left. Walk down the steps. You will see the terracotta floor of an old pavilion on your right. Go down the roughly hewn flag stones, do take care as they are worn. Continue along the path, now with the railing on the right, and cross over the bridge, spanning the Chelt, and then turn right. Cross over a second bridge, past a sun dial and a rectangular pond in the formal style with fountains and water lilies. Leave Sandford park, at the Bath Road, and turn right. Cross the road at the controlled crossing, by the Crown and Cushion on the corner of Vernon Place, and continue up to the High Street. Turn left at the top and you are now back on the circular walk.

Walk back along the pedestrianised area and turn left into Cambray Place.

Sandford Park

Point 16. Cambray Place

When the Duke of Wellington came to Cheltenham after the battle of Waterloo, the town was illuminated in his honour and triumphal arches of welcome were erected across the High Street at Cambray Place. He stayed here as a guest of Colonel Riddell. Dr Thomas Cristie lived at number 1, he was a pupil of Dr Jenner, the pioneer of vaccination. The Baptist Church, on the right, was designed by Henry Dangerfield in the Italian Renaissance style. Walk down towards the Cambray Court Flats and take the path on the right into Rodney Road and turn right.

Point 17. Rodney Road and the Lloyds Bank Building

Look at the beautiful ironwork and railing, of the many terraces, on the left side of the road. Number 15 and 17 have the more unusual iron work known as the "web" design. Rodney Lodge was built by Robert Hughes, son of the owner of the Assembly rooms. It is an impressive two storeyed house and has a Greek Ionic porch.

The imposing Lloyds Bank building, dating from 1900, stands on the site of the assembly rooms which were originally opened in 1816 by the Duke of Wellington on one of his many visits to the town. The rules and regulations of the Assembly rooms of 1816 may amuse the twentieth century visitor. That the public amusements for the Summer Season are as follows:

***

Monday: Ball and Cards
Wednesday: Ladies Promenade and Card assembly
Friday: Ball and Cards

***

That gentleman can not be admitted to the ball in boots
or half boots; officers in their uniforms excepted.
That no hazard, or game of chance,
be on any account
permitted in these rooms.

***

Ten years later the rules have become yet more strict.

***

The style and well regulated order of society in
Cheltenham is not its slightest recommendation ...
and it is the singular good fortune and justly proud boast
of our town that among its patrons are included the first
personages of the country, in station, affluence and
respectability; whilst no unprivileged footstep is
suffered to intrude upon the circle of their pleasures.

***

As you approach the High Street imagine how it would have been when prim-roses and violets grew between cottages roofed in thatch. The diverted stream trickled through the street and stepping stones allowed people to cross over this offensive open sewer. On three days of each week mill own-ers were ordered to sluice the area in order to clean the street. The unwary visitor could slip into the water up to the knee. In the sixteenth century, it became necessary to pass a law controlling the roaming of dogs in the High Street This old record of 1576 states that:

***

It is ordered that any man that will keep a mastiff dog
or bitch that he shall keep him muzzled or tied up,
for there can not go into the streets neither man,
women nor child nor beast nor pig
with out hurt or danger of life ...
and there for desiring you Mr Steward
to see some good order to be taken therein,
or else there is no man nor beast can escape
that shall be devoured with these Mastiffs
that be in the town of Cheltenham.

***

Turn left by the Lloyds building, into the High Street. It was first paved in 1787 and was lit by 120 oil lamps which were attended to by one lamp lighter

Point 18. The Regent Arcade

The Regent Arcade now stands where the Plough Hotel, the old coaching inn, once stood. Much of the facade closely resembles the original judging from a picture of the Plough Hotel painted in 1870 by John C. Maggs of Bath, which can be seen in the Art Gallery. The stable yards, accommodating one hundred horses, a number of coach houses with dove cotes above and granaries to hold 5000 bushels, stood at the back of the Inn which now forms the shopping arcade.

In its heyday the Inn was the heart of the town and 30 to 40 "coach & four" travelled along the high street each day going on to Bath or London. With the introduction of Turnpike roads between 1785 and 1825 the journey to the Metropolis could be completed in ten and a half hours. The centre for travel in Cheltenham moved from the Plough Inn to Malvern station where, for a short time in the 1930's, the Cheltenham Flyer was the fastest train in Britain, completing the journey to London in 2 hours and 23 and a half minutes. Now turn into Regent Arcade.

Point 19. The Wishing Fish Clock

The unique clock, inside the Regent Arcade, was designed and constructed by Kit Williams and is very popular with children. When the hour is sounded the fish suspended under the clock revolves as it blows out bubbles and plays such popular tunes as "The Sun Has Got its Hat On" and "I'm forever Blowing Bubbles" for your entertainment. Catch a bubble and make a wish!

The clock is believed to be the world's tallest mechanical clock at 45 feet (almost 14 metres).

Walk down to the bottom of the arcade, turn right, through the glass doors and out into Ormond Place. Turn right into Regent Street, under the glass covered bridge, and walk along to the canopied entrance of the Everyman theatre.

Point 20. The Everyman Theatre and Regent Street

The New Theatre and Opera House which became the Everyman theatre, was opened on 1st October 1891. Lillie Langtry, who was known as "Jersey Lillie", brought her own company down from the Princess Theatre, London, to perform for the people of the town. At one time the theatre was used to show films. The building was designed by Frank Matcham and is red brick with stone dressings, inside you will find a "very elaborate rococo lastowash decoration to the front of galleries." In 1960 the Opera House became the Everyman Theatre. The Richardson studio, in the theatre, is a memorial to Sir Ralph Richardson, the actor, who was closely connected with the town. On the corner of County Court Road is the court building. Notice the tops of the railings with their lion heads.

This proud looking Lion is just one of many you can find on the railings surrounding the County Court

Continue onto the paved area at the top of the road. Look out for the decorative heads atop the ground floor windows on the right. Turn left and walk back to the Midland Bank building. This now completes our circular walk.

We hope you have enjoyed "The Cheltenham Experience" and that you have discovered a little of what this great spa town has to offer the visitor.

Have you successfully completed the quiz? The answers can be found on page 32.

Please look for others in this series "The Cirencester Experience" and "The Burford Experience".

Bibliography

Book of Cheltenham (The) by Steven Blake and Roger Beacham.
Published by Barracuda Books
Cheltenham, A Biography. By Simona Pakenham.
Published by Macmillian London Ltd.
Cheltenham. by Bryan Little. Published by B.T. Batsford Ltd
Cheltenham Companion (A) by Alwyn Sampson and Steven Blake.
Published by Portico Press.
Cheltenham in Old Photographs, collected by Roger Whiting.
Published in 1986 by Alan Sutton.
Cheltenham in Old Photographs, A Second Selection,
collected by Roger Whiting. Published in 1988 by Alan Sutton.
Cheltenham's Ornamental Ironwork. by Amina Chatwin and
Published by the author.
History of Cheltenham (A) by Gwen Hart.
Published by Alan Sutton Publishing Ltd.
Norman's History of Cheltenham, by John Goding.
Published by Longman.
Pleasure Town, Cheltenham 1830-1860. By Arthur Bell.
Published by Richard Sadler Ltd.

Like two sentinels these lamps are mounted on stone pillars at the foot of the steps leading up into the Municipal Offices

Answers to the Cheltenham Experience Quiz

A.   Stone carvings of game, fur and feather.

B.   Six red telephone boxes.

C.   Four iron Lamp Posts with a ring of pigeons around the centre.

D.   Six floral garlands carved in stone.

E.   Twelve Crowns over window arches.

F.   A Caryatid standing between Janet Herring's dress shop windows.

G.   One has her right knee forward and the other the left.

H.   The Lion on the Rotunda.

I.   A Pestle and Mortar outside the chemist's shop.

J.   Four. The others hang over the rim !

K.   36 Arches. Two x eighteen.

L.   The John Dower House.

M.   The Electric sub-station. 1895.

N.   The Library and Shakespeare.

O.   Six unique bay windows in three matching pairs.

P.   Nine. Seven large and two small Urns on top of the Lloyd's building.

Q.   The Bradford & Bingley building. Also the Clock and Weather Vane.

R.   Rodney Hall.

S.   Rodney Lodge.

T.   Wishing Fish Clock.